The Financial Sherpa

The Financial Sherpa

Copyright © 2015 by Jon P. Voyles Sr.

Printed in the United States of America
ISBN 13: 978-1511931809
ISBN 10: 1511931809

Table of Contents

ACKNOWLEDGMENTS

Rusty, thank you for your friendship, mentorship, the slow jazz and the long walks on the beach. Your fatherly advice has always been invaluable. Thank you for sharing ALL of your wisdom, which was 37 seconds well spent.

But joking aside and in all honesty, in the writing of this book I realized that it really became a way to honor you for all that you have taught me. Thanks!

Chapter 1

8:28 am, at the office of Associates Insurance agency in Loveland, Colorado.

Ok, thank you Phil, I will get that certificate of insurance off to your general contractor as soon as we get off the phone. Thanks again for your business!

Joe?

Yes Sharon?

You have a voice mail that came in from an Aaron from some company in Arkansas. They want to talk to you about marketing some financial product to seniors?

Ok thanks, I will check that out.

Press 1 to hear your messages...Mr. Patrick, my name is Aaron Childress from Retirement Solutions and I wanted to talk to you about helping seniors with retirement planning. Please call me back at 800-555-1212.

Sharon!

Yes Joe?

Could you please listen to this voicemail and do some background research on that company. I am intrigued but am tired of all the sales calls to the office. I have enough on my plate running a commercial insurance agency. Not sure I can add another product to the lineup.

No problem!

I need to get Phil's certificate off right away as I promised.

2 hours later, after many interruptions and other tasks...

Joe?

2

Yes, Sharon.

Here is that information on Retirement Solutions that you asked for. They seem like a legitimate company, but why are you interested in this?

Sharon, as you know we have been doing this insurance gig for quite some time and you also know I am very skeptical about any and all of the sales calls that we get about this company or that one wanting us to market their stuff. But for some reason this call just got my attention and I feel like I should call the guy and hear him out.

Wow, something must have clicked because usually you just hang up on these guys!

Ya, I know. My people skills are lacking most of the time, especially when it comes to telemarketers.

Couple of days later...

Hello, this is Aaron with Retirement Solutions, how may I help you?

Aaron, this is Joe Patrick in Colorado. You called my office a few days back and I finally found about 5 minutes to hear what it is you were referring to when it came to helping seniors...I got that right didn't I?

Yes, you did! And thanks for returning my call. Joe, we have been working with the senior market for quite some time and have found that they are really needing our help. They have been given some great sales pitches over the years but sales pitches don't keep them from running out of money!

Ain't that the truth!

It really is Joe, and here is the kicker, most of them don't really know where to turn or what is even the best plan of attack to keep them from running out of money, or giving it all to Medicaid or the government.

Why not the government? They are frugal and conscientious about every dime they spend aren't they?

That's a good one Joe. I can see that you see the need for some gut level honesty regarding money. These people need our help but unfortunately they are taken advantage of all too often.

I hate that. It makes me sick.

Me too Joe, and that is why I created Retirement Solutions, to help shed some light and help others. Beautiful thing about it is that I make a decent living helping others and I would guess that you feel the same way about Associates Insurance?

Sure do! I founded this agency from my own blood, sweat and tears...mostly tears, *ha*. But I found that my hometown really needed someone that they could turn to for honest answers and could trust for their insurance needs.

That's great Joe, sounds like we are of a similar mindset. Let me ask you, what do you really know about money?

That I don't ever seem to have enough!

I hear ya! But do you really understand how money works?

Just what they taught me in school.

So absolutely nothing then!

Exactly!

Don't feel bad because you are not alone. Most people graduate high school not even knowing what a budget is, let alone how to stay within one.

And most of them went straight to Congress!

True. Sadly, our society has been given poor, misleading and erroneous information and they are basing all of their future on this info. Let me put it to you this way, what if everything you thought you knew about money was wrong? Scary thought, huh?

Definitely!

So let me ask you this, if everything you thought you knew about money was wrong, how soon would you want to know?

Yesterday, 20 years ago, at birth! I mean obviously I would want to know as soon as possible.

Exactly, and that is what we offer our clients, truth. Not sales pitches, but harsh reality truth.

This sounds good, please elaborate.

How much time do you have?

Well now that you mention it, I am cutting it close today, and I promised my wife that I would actually have dinner with her...and not be late again. Can we reschedule?

Great, sounds good to me.

Chapter 2

Good morning Joe, this is Aaron. Did I catch you at a good time?

Good morning to you too Aaron, actually you did. Just finishing up with some work but I am at a good stopping point.

Great, do you want to pick up where we left off?

Yes, been thinking a lot about what you said. If everything I knew about money were wrong, how soon would I want to know. That really stuck with me.

That's why I asked. But let's start from the basics. Do you have a financial advisor Joe?

I do, but only because he worked with me on a company plan 401k that I had from before I started my agency.

And how long had it been since you spoke with him.

I started my agency 7 years ago.

Long pause…..

Are you telling me that it's been 7 years since you have spoken to your advisor?

Well, yes. I mean I get a Christmas card from him once a year but we haven't really had anything to discuss for a while. All of my extra money has been tied up in building this agency.

So your financial plan is an old 401k from a previous employer and the agency you are building, is that about it?

No, I have a couple of old 401k's from jobs before that last one and some savings. Oh, and I also add some money to that 401k or IRA whatever it is from time to time when I can. It depends on what my CPA recommends.

Ok, do you have any life insurance?

I do. I have a 10 year term policy that I started 3 years ago for $250,000.

And do you have a mortgage?

Yes, I do. I owe about $200,000 on my loan.

If you don't mind me asking, what is the current value of your home?

Aaron, I am not sure how any of this has to do with me not knowing about money and the senior market.

If you will just humor me, I promise you that even though the questions are going to get deeper you will see how it all ties together. Trust me enough to go a little further?

Well, I don't know you, but sure. I think based on what the houses are selling for around me my home has a value of about $300,000.

Ok, now this may sound weird but we need to discuss your home owners and auto insurance.

Ok Aaron, now you have lost me. How does that apply to money and my understanding of it?

That's a fair question. Let me explain. I am sure you have flown in a plane, right?

Sure, plenty of times.

Great, if you have ever looked out the window, you get to see some amazing things. But what is intriguing is that you get to see what others on the ground don't. As an example, you can look at a road and see that there are curves up ahead or a dead end, or even a crossroads. But from the driver's seat of the car, you can only see a short distance in front of you, make sense?

Sure.

Ok, your financial life is very similar.

How is that?

You have already told me that you have a banker, a CPA, a financial advisor, a real estate agent, an insurance agent. That's what we refer to as micro advisors. You are limited by utilizing an advisor for any part of your financial life if they can't see what's ahead. It they aren't a macro advisor they are sitting next to you in the car, without a map.

I guess that makes sense.

We all have these "experts" in our life, helping us with different areas regarding finances and protection, but when is the last time you ever had all of them in the same room, sitting around a table to discuss your finances.

Well, never. Who does?

Most don't but that is my point. How can you be sure that one person's advice doesn't conflict with another's?

Good point, I guess I have never thought about that. Is it like a doctor who will look at your file to be sure that he doesn't prescribe something that could interact with another prescription and could kill you?

Exactly. You are catching on quickly Joe. But here is the scary part, almost all of us have micro planners in our life that help us navigate around, but without a macro planner to oversee all the dead ends, twists, turns, and crossroads how do we have any confidence that we really have a plan? Or that we will get where we are going.

Now you are scaring me.

As I should. You are only scared because you are now thinking about your own financial life and realizing at some point you have been driving with a blindfold on.

Ya, no kidding. But I guess to answer the insurance question, what do you need to know?

First off, what are your deductibles for both the home and auto coverages?

I was struggling when I got started so I put on the lowest dollar amount of coverage that I could and since I knew that I have very little savings, I put a $250 deductible on everything.

Fair enough, now Joe I need you to understand something here, I am not trying to make you question your decisions, or feel bad about them. I am simply trying to get a macro view of your financial life, fair enough?

Sure.

Great, so your home is covered for how much?

$300,000

Ok, and your autos?

I never felt comfortable with the basic coverage so I went above state minimums and put $50,000/$100,000/$25,000 on the autos. Again, to save money.

Ok, do you have any teenage drivers?

My daughter is 17. Great kid with straight A's and a very good driver.

Well that is winning half the battle right there isn't it?

You can say that again.

Ok, do you have any umbrella coverage?

No.

Ok, do you have a will?

No.

Does your wife work?

Actually my agency is getting to the place where we don't need her income and she is going to quit in August and just be mom.

Great for her. Does she have any life insurance?

Yes she does. She has a group plan with her work for $150,000.

Ok, now I could continue in this line of questioning but I have some good news, and some bad news...

Chapter 3

Wendy!

I'm in the laundry room Joe.

Hey babe, how was your day?

It was good, and yours?

Well I finally got that bowling alley to sign up that I had quoted and a few other new clients today.

Well that's awesome! I am proud of you, guess my days as a bookkeeper are numbered.

Interesting that you brought that up. Do you remember me telling you about that guy in Arkansas that I spoke with about retirement plans?

Sure.

Well we had a long talk today and he really opened my eyes up with some very thought provoking questions.

Are we broke?

Not yet. But he wants me to go talk with a friend of his in Colorado Springs that has been very successful. He said that this guy really understands how money works and how I could use that information in my agency as well as in our finances.

What are they selling?

Well that is the interesting part, so far nothing. But he is trying to help me see finances, and I quote, from a 30,000 foot view.

Well I guess it doesn't hurt to at least talk. But you don't normally talk to these guys. What is different about this guy?

You are right about that. I guess what got me was a question that he asked me and that was, "what training and/or education have we been given in life, whether from school or jobs, that makes me wise concerning our finances?" I know that I didn't have classes either in high school or college to help me, did you?

No.

And he asked me, what if everything I thought I knew about money were wrong, how soon would I want to know.

That's kind of scary.

That's what I said. If you are in agreement I am going to schedule an appointment with this guy he calls the "Financial Sherpa".

Well that doesn't sound weird. But why do you need me there? You normally handle all of the money stuff

He said that you had to be there, it's a family thing. And that if you weren't that the Sherpa guy would just reschedule.

Ok, let's go look at the calendar.

Chapter 4

Good morning, this is Clarence.

Clarence, my name is Joe Patrick and I got your name and number from Aaron Childress at Retirement Solutions in Arkansas.

Yes, he sent me an email telling me a little about you.

He suggested that I give you a call regarding my finances and how I could advise my clients utilizing your strategies.

Great, when do you and your wife want to sit down and talk?

Isn't there just something that you can send me to review first?

Ok, let me get this straight, you just want me to send you some literature? How is that any different from what you have already been given in the past? I mean, when you get your yearly statement from your financial advisor, do you review every chart and graph and compare that to your plan to determine if you are on track for retirement? Then cross reference that to your bank statements, your will, and your insurance statements?

Well, no.

And you would be like almost every other person walking the face of the earth. It would just be more paperwork. I want to help you to understand that every decision, or lack thereof, affects every other decision regarding your financial life.

Is this all about that 30,000 foot view again?

It sure is, but there is more to it than that. When is that last time you sat down with your financial advisor?

7 years ago.

7 years?! Let me ask you, has anything in your life changed in 7 years? Your jobs, your age, anything?

Well of course it has.

Then I have to ask, and this is as much your responsibility as your advisor's, why are you not getting together on a regular basis to ensure that the recommendations from 7 years ago are still valid today? The likely answer is because we are all lazy regarding our finances. Do you think that someone like a Donald Trump or a Warren Buffet only looks at his portfolio once every 7 years?

Of course not.

Then can we agree that it is time to look under the hood to see if you need any scheduled maintenance or even a tune up?

No, you are right, its time.

Chapter 5

Colorado Springs, Colorado
Clarence Walsh home office
3:00 pm

Wow Wendy, look at that house!

Ya, apparently this guy is the Financial Guru or whatever it is you called him.

Financial Sherpa.

What does that even mean?

Not sure but we will find out.

Morning! Come on in, my name is Clarence but everyone calls me Rusty.

Hi Rusty. I'm Joe Patrick and this is my wife Wendy.

Wow Joe, you married up!

Thanks. I think so.

Ok you two, stop making me blush.

So guys, how can I help you?

Aaron told us that you were someone that could help us to understand how money works.

Well, that is the rumor.

We are curious about what this process is that you and Aaron are talking about. It is interesting but the pieces aren't lining up just yet in our minds.

Ok, Aaron sent me the information that you and he talked about regarding your current financial status, and I have reviewed it and would like to go deeper, if that is ok with you.

Sure, that's why we are here.

Great. Here is the information that Aaron sent me.

Joe 40 healthy non smoker
Wendy 38 healthy non smoker

Home value $300000 loan $200000 insured for $300000 with a $250 deductible

Joe life insurance $250,000
Wendy life insurance $150,000 (soon to be zero)

Auto coverage 50/100/25 $250 deductible

Joes IRA's 200,000
Wendy's IRA 125,000
Savings 12000

No Will
No umbrella

17 year old daughter

Self employed

Does that sound about right?

Sure does all except the soon to be zero on Wendy's life insurance. I never said that.

Ok, I will explain that when we get there. But I have to ask, do you see any issues with your existing plan? Are you comfortable where you are?

Well, I can only speak for me and not Wendy, but aside from wanting more in savings and wishing I had more invested, we feel we are on track.

Wendy, do you agree with Joe?

Pretty much, just wish we had more saved up.

If you could change anything, would you?

Maybe a few things, but I feel we are on track.

Joe, you have said a couple of times that you are on track. What track is that? I mean what does your track look like, and where is it going? And how will you know when you have arrived?

Rusty, that is always the million dollar question for everyone, but I would guess that a million dollars would be great. Wendy?

I don't even know. I guess I'm just relying on Joe to make those decisions.

Well guys, you aren't any different than most of America and as a matter of fact, you are better off than most Americans. But as the saying goes, be careful where you are headed because you may end up where you are going. As I look at your finances, I see several major issues and a few minor adjustments.

Like?

We will get there I promise, but I am trying to see what I am dealing with first. Here is what I mean by that, if you don't see a problem, then it would be very difficult for me to provide you a solution. Wouldn't you agree?

Well, yes.

Ok, so what I am going to do is take your financial life apart piece by piece in order to show you how the pieces of the puzzle interact. Are you guys ready for the ride?

Sure.

Alright, fasten your seat belts.

Chapter 6

Let's start with the basics. What do you think I do for a living and how does it affect you?

Well I would say that you are an expert on knowing about investments and what would make money and help us to diversify our portfolio. Wendy?

I guess that about sums it up.

Ok, let me tell you a story.

Bursting the Bubbles

Generally, your socio-economic background, your education and mostly your skill set will determine how much money you will earn. This amount of money will determine your lifestyle, and depending on your personality, you will either be a saver or a spender. Those that are spenders usually amass debt along with that lifestyle and can find themselves a slave to their debt.

Then there are savers. Savers go to a financial planner to discuss how they can invest their money. Most planners will discuss three basic principles with them and using any two of those principles, he can determine the third.

They are:
- *Money*
- *Time*
- *Risk*

Here is that basic 8th grade algebraic formula. The planner will tell you to either lower your lifestyle to give him more money to work with, lengthen the time to retirement so that you can give the money time to grow, or take more risk with your money that could either shorten or indefinitely extend your time to retirement. Any or all of these factors are very volatile and yet he will put together these factors and bundle them all up in a nice little leather binder and charge you $2500 dollars.

But there is another area that comes into play that dramatically affects your finances and how much you will have at retirement, Taxes and Insurance. These are a drain on your finances, and if you don't prepare in this area properly, could be catastrophic to your retirement. The picture looks rather bleak at this point but it doesn't have to be with a properly planned financial life. What you need is someone who understands the taxes and insurances side of the equation and how it can also directly and indirectly affect the investment piece of the puzzle.

So, does that part make sense to you guys?

I think it does, because Wendy and I realized that we needed to take control of the financial picture otherwise there may not be a picture. On the spending side for example, Wendy noticed that we picked up an ugly habit, Starbucks, and this habit was costing us anywhere from $3 to $12 dollars daily depending on if I had to meet clients there. Once we added up how much we were spending on coffee it was shocking to realize that several hundred dollars a year we were…excuse the phrase, but pissing away. This caused us to look closer and realize that we were just being lazy. We could brew coffee at home, much cheaper. So we took the step to make that a treat or an exception and not the rule.

Wow, that is great to hear. Not because I don't like Starbucks because I have that nasty little habit myself, but what it shows me is that you are pliable and want to focus on the future and not just the immediate gratification that plagues most of us daily. Besides getting away from the spender mentality, there are several other common misconceptions that we need to address. Is investing in stocks and bonds the only way to amass a retirement?

I hope not because one reason that I started my agency was to build it up to be able to sell it or my daughter take it over someday as a way to retire.

Well that is good to hear Joe, it tells me that you are thinking outside of the conventional box of thinking and looking for other options. Wendy, what about you? You are being rather quiet.

Oh, I am just trying to keep up and digest all that you are discussing. There is a lot to take in.

There sure is.

But to answer your question, we have always discussed how nice it would be to have some property or properties in another state, like Florida, Texas or New Mexico that we could both vacation at and then rent them out when we aren't there.

That is a great idea you guys. Have you been looking?

No, it's always just been a pipe dream at this point.

Ok Joe. Would you agree with Wendy on this point?

We are close to the same page, but I was always leery of getting into the real estate side of things because what if the water heater bursts or something like that and I am 1000 miles away.

Great question, but that is why you use a property management company and be sure to look at properties with a professional realtor. Not just anyone but a solid performer that knows their stuff and has been a landlord, so that they can help you know your total overall costs and if a property will make money or make a money pit. I have some references of people that I work with in that arena. This brings up another great point. When working with me, I will refer you to other professionals that I have aligned myself with because from a macro view I need them to help create a plan that will work for you.

Ok Rusty, I have a random question.

And what would that be Wendy?

What is a Financial Sherpa?

HA! So Aaron told you about that.

Yes he did.

Well, we will get into that in a bit. In order for it to make any sense, we need to keep assembling this puzzle. Before we move on, you understand that there are other ways to build wealth by simply looking outside the traditional investment bubble, right?

Yes.

Me too.

Great.

Chapter 7

Joe, let me ask you a rather tough question.

Ok.

When you took the licensing exam for insurance, did it teach you anything about coverages, deductibles, etc?

It taught me what covers what, is that what you mean?

Not exactly, when you wrote insurance on your home and auto, what parameters did you use in deciding coverage?

I did it based on what I could afford.

Joe, can I be honest with you?

Sure.

Based on my experience, you did what most Americans do, and that is buy insurance the way the insurance company's market insurance to them. Buy it as cheap as you can. But there is a reason for that. Do you know why?

Well I am a little embarrassed to say, not really.

Its ok Joe, I am not here to beat you up but rather to educate and help you. Most insurance companies want to sell a policy where they have the least amount of exposure to risk for the highest price possible. Wouldn't you agree?

Sure.

And here is how they do it, they sell on price and price alone. I am sure you've seen the commercials. So for instance, your auto insurance, you have just above the state minimums required to have coverage in the state of Colorado, but let's look at it from a completely different and very scary side. The exposure and litigation side. If you are only covered for $25,000 property damage, that means that if you or your family is at fault in an accident, you only have enough coverage to pay for a cheap SUV, so whatever you do, do NOT hit a Mercedes. Does that make sense?

Yes.

Ok, it gets worse. If you look at your bodily injury side, you are only covered for $50,000 per person and $100,000 per accident, do you know what that covers in a hospital today? It buys you 2 aspirin and an X-ray. I am trying to make jokes here but it really isn't a laughing matter to people who have been in accidents.

I get what you are saying and am embarrassed to say that I never thought about it from that stand point. When I put that coverage in place, it was to save us money when I started the agency, but I guess it's time to reevaluate my coverage.

Good, I appreciate your willingness to be receptive here Joe, because I know that it is tough to look at this. Unfortunately I am not done.

Oh great.

I don't see that you have any kind of an umbrella coverage.

No we don't have that.

Can I suggest that you look at getting some? Especially with a teenage driver in your home. Most carriers you can get a policy pretty cheap for $1,000,000 and that covers you above and beyond your limits for the car insurance.

I will do that.

Great, now let me explain that the right way to protect yourself with insurance isn't by paying the least but by putting the insurance company on the hook for the highest amount of coverage that you can.

Sounds expensive.

Ok, let's talk cost. If there were a law passed in Colorado tomorrow that states that the most you be liable for in any accident would be $2500, would you still have auto insurance?

No.

Why?

I would simply self-insure because I have at least that in my savings account.

Very good Joe! You are much smarter than Wendy says you are.

Ha ha.

But you are right, you wouldn't insure yourself for all of that exposure, but unfortunately the state didn't pass that law. But if you build your insurance policy correctly, you will still only be liable for the same $2500.

You are referring to the deductible.

Yes. If you increase your limits of coverage on your policy, it will increase your premiums, but the way to lower the premiums is to put yourself at risk for the highest deductible and put away your portion of the exposure in an account and then having the highest deductible on your policy thereby providing you with the most coverage at the smallest premium possible.

That makes sense, but they don't teach you this stuff on the test.

You are right, but fortunately this is a curve or twist in the road that we can avoid by insuring yourself for the proper coverage.

Thinking macro again.

That is exactly right Wendy.

Chapter 8

Ok, next on the agenda is to look at your coverage for your greatest asset.

Our home?

Sorry Wendy no, any ideas Joe?

Probably our investments.

You are both close but not quite the right answer. I am referring to your single greatest asset that once it is gone, there is no way to replace it. An asset that makes it possible to have all of the other assets.

Our life?

Yes Wendy, but specifically it is your ability to earn an income. I want you to really get this, this is very important. So important that it directly and indirectly affects every single part of your financial plan. You have a home because you have talents and abilities that allow you to be a productive member of society and generate an income. This income is where everything comes from, your home, your auto, your toys, and heck even your ability to have investments like a 401k comes directly from your ability to earn an income. If you are gone due to an early demise, your income earning potential stops, your creativity stops, everything stops. But there are others who are still here trying to pick up where you left off.

I guess I hadn't thought about it that way.

Most don't Joe, but I want you to think about this. Your greatest asset is the ability to earn an income and if you are gone, you can leave your legacy by making sure that you create a self-completion to your financial plan. For example, I will use simple math here so that I don't confuse myself.

Joe you are 40 yrs. old and you probably have at least 30 good years left in you to be productive, right?

Sure, I guess.

Ok, let's say you earn just $50,000 a year with no raises for that entire time period. That is 50,000 x 30 or a 1,500,000 dollar impact on your family over your lifetime at 70 years old. This is only your financial impact, but you see the simple math that if something were to happen to you, your family misses out on far more than your good looks! It is cheated out of 1.5 million ways that you can leave a legacy.

Wow, I guess I never realized that.

Me neither.

Guys, this is why my job is so important. Even if Wendy were to remarry, wouldn't you rather leave her with the choice to marry rather than forcing her to make a choice based on poor planning? I don't like to refer to it as life insurance but rather love insurance.

And I definitely love her.

I can see that you do, and that is why this is important. My concern is that you only have a term policy for $250,000, so we will need to address this as well, fair enough?

Sounds good.

Wendy, I want to talk to you about your coverage. When are you planning on leaving your job?

End of August.

Ok, are you aware of your options available to you once you leave your group coverage for your life insurance?

I don't know. I hadn't really thought much about it.

Ok, let me enlighten you to the options. The insurance company bases its risk exposure on a group policy solely on the law of large numbers, meaning that they don't underwrite you based on your health but rather on the probability of you dying based solely on your sex, age group and other factors. When you leave your job, you don't get to take that same coverage with and usually they will offer some form of permanent coverage to replace it. But since they don't really have a good indicator of you as a risk they will offer you the product that costs the most since you are a higher risk to them. So you are paying the most for the worst, and that is what I meant by soon to be zero when we discussed your current financial status. Next we should discuss that from our previous example you can probably surmise that you are low on coverage as well.

We figured that since Joe was the main bread winner that he wouldn't need as much money if I were to die.

Most people think along those lines but I have to tell you that I have been in this business long enough that I have seen what happens when someone loses a spouse. You heard him say that he definitely loves you earlier right?

Yes.

And that was unprompted by my so he is probably telling the truth.

You are going to make me cry.

Don't worry, I have tissues. *Ha ha,* but I need you both to consider something. This isn't just about replacing income. If something were to happen to you Wendy, I am willing to bet that Joe will need a little time. Here is what I mean, if you were to die, do you think that it would affect Joe's ability to make an income at his job?

Ya, I guess.

You bet it would, he would be a basket case for days, weeks, and months. There is no way that he would be at the top of his game and business would suffer. He might even need to hire someone to help out for a while so that he can get his life in order. Life insurance simply buys him some time to grieve.

Ok, you got me, stop it....can you hand me some tissues?

Not a problem, we can stop there, but one last thing to think about.

Really? You are going to make me cry more?

No, but I need you to realize that Russian Brides are expensive and Joe will need the money....

Room erupts with laughter

And Joe, Wendy will have to get a pool boy and possibly install a pool so that the neighbors don't talk.

More laughter

This is an area where I can help you guys save some money so we need to keep this in mind. Not cheaper insurance but better insurance, right Joe?

Right!

Chapter 9

Let's address that cheaper insurance for a moment. Joe, what is the cheapest life insurance out there?

Term insurance.

That's exactly right, but why is it the cheapest?

I guess it's because there is a time limit on the coverage so the insurance company is only on the hook for a potential payout for a limited time.

You are correct Joe, and here are the statistics. Did you know that roughly less than 2% of all term policies sold will ever pay a death benefit? That is why they are so cheap, they are a cash cow for the insurance companies. You pay them but rarely will they pay your beneficiaries.

I guess that makes sense.

Really? Less than 2%?

Wendy, the numbers vary depending on who is giving you that statistic but regardless of the source, it's a very small percentage and always less than 3%.

We are in the wrong business Joe. We should be insuring people.

No kidding.

Ok, guys here is another myth. We have been told for years to "Buy Term and Invest the Difference". Sounds like a good plan, right? Who said it first? Where did it come from? How does it work? And does it work?

Hopefully you have these answers Rusty.

It is a sales technique that has been around for decades and it was a way to generate or churn business for insurance agents during the slow times with people who had permanent policies. Only issue is, it doesn't work for the long haul.

Then why do people do it?

They don't really know any better and it doesn't help when you have some great authors, speakers, radio and talk show hosts who have made a ton of money telling you that you should buy term and invest the difference. I am here to tell you that only a small portion of the time will it ever make sense, and you don't want to be in that percentage otherwise Wendy will need more tissues.

Stop it Rusty.

Sorry Wendy, but I would have to ask you the question. Even if you are a religious believer in buy term and invest the difference, are you doing it? All of it?

What do you mean all of it?

Are you buying term and then investing the difference?

No, I bought term and invested in groceries.

Guys, I get it. Please don't misunderstand me, there is a place for term insurance, there is a time, but rarely should that be your only insurance. I get people coming into my office all the time needing insurance and some of them are not springs chickens. One thing to keep in mind is that the more successful you are, the more you have to lose. But I will stop because we will get into how all of this works later. For now, can we agree that you will be open to discussion?

Yes, definitely.

Yes.

Good, nuf said!

Chapter 10

Ok, let's look at some other areas of your current plan.

I notice that you each have some 401k/IRA money. Tell me a little about that.

I'll go first because it is simple. I am investing in my 401k at work and will do so until August, if I leave then. I'm having second thoughts after this conversation if it's wise to quit.

Ok thanks Wendy, couple of questions. Does your employer match your 401k?

There is a match up to 3% but I have to put in 5% to get the full match.

Ok great, are you taking full advantage?

And then some, I am actually putting in 10%.

Really? What is your reasoning for that decision?

Why is that wrong?

I didn't say that, I just want to better understand your thoughts and reasons for your decision is all.

Well I figured if I didn't need the money to live on, then I would take the tax break for putting money into the 401k.

Tax break?

Ya, the tax break.

Ok Joe, lets discuss yours.

Well I had a couple of different jobs before the insurance agency and the 401k's were doing pretty good where they were, so I didn't move them. I moved the one from my last job because like I said, it was the guy who was taking care of my 401k so I rolled it to an IRA with him after I left. I periodically put money in for that same reason that Wendy mentioned. And it has paid off, I got a 10% return last year. See, right here.

Ok good, let's take a look at that statement. So you said you received a 10% return last year, that's pretty good.

Ya, we were happy.

So did you contribute to the IRA last year?

Sure did.

I see that, so I am just doing some quick math here and by looking at your statement, I am not coming up with the same Rate of Return.

What do you mean?

I mean that your return is closer to 2% than it is 10.

No, look at the ending balance.

I see that but that is including your contributions and your return, that isn't your return. When you subtract out your contributions, your return is closer to 2%

I feel stupid.

Why? I wouldn't expect you to know how to read this but what I am concerned about is that in the last 7 years your advisor hasn't taken the time to explain this to you. We can discuss rates of return in a bit, but I want to get back to the tax break discussion. Why do you feel that you are getting a tax break by investing in a 401k or an IRA?

Well that's just what we were told when they set it up. Invest money in now, get the tax break and then in your retirement years, you will be in a lower tax bracket.

Do you believe that?

I thought I did, but now I am questioning myself.

Then we are on the right track. Every decision you make regarding finances should not only be put on trial, but put on trial for its life. What I mean by that is, does this decision make sense not just today but in the future. But let's take that even further, will it make sense if things change.

What things?

Well Joe, let's discuss for a moment the tax break myth.

Myth?

Yes Wendy, myth. The notion that there is a tax break today and a tax break tomorrow is not how our government works. Do they ever do anything that has your best interest in mind, or theirs?

Theirs...*in unison.*

You are right. However, when 401k's were first introduced, that strategy actually worked. In the early 80's there were 15 different tax brackets with the highest bracket being 75%. Today we have 6 brackets and the highest is 39.6%. But not only that, a person making $100,000 in those days could defer paying taxes on $20,000 worth of income putting it in a 401k and they would drop 2 tax brackets by doing it. They would go from 59% to 49%, and that same person today could live comfortably on that same $80,000 in a 28% tax bracket. So it made sense. However, today if you defer $20,000 worth of income from your $100,000, you will drop how many tax brackets?

One?

No Joe, it's a round number, it is zero, that's right you will not get any tax break for deferring that income and not paying your taxes on it, but here is a scary proposition. We are in a low income tax environment right now. What happens if taxes go up?

Well shoot, I guess we lose.

You are correct, but I need to ask you a question, do you see taxes going up, down or staying that same?

We discussed it, we see them going up.

That's right Joe, and if you are correct, you deferred paying taxes on your income at 28% so that you could pay at 38, 48, 88%?

Rusty! 88%? Come on!

Did you know that historically the highest tax brackets have been in the 90% range?

Really?

Holy smokes!

Exactly, and I also want to point out that there are many other flaws with investing in these products too. We don't need to get into all of them, but just know that if you invest here, you are under all of the rules and regulations of the IRS and they don't play well with others.

We know that!

I am going to make you guys an offer. I will loan you money, no credit check, no collateral, and just 2 conditions. First, I will tell you what the interest rate will be when I need it. Second, I will tell you the terms of the loan when I need you to repay the money. How much money would you like me to loan you?

No one would take that deal Rusty.

You already have.

Huh?

These are the terms of any of those type of plans. They can change the tax rates on you at any time and they can change how it's paid back. For instance, you cannot access that money prior to 59 ½ without a penalty of 10% and whatever the tax rates are at that time. But did you know that if you don't need the money that you have to take it anyways?

Really?

Yes, it's called RMD or Required Minimum Distribution and what it states is that if you don't take the required distributions by age 70 ½ you will be hit with a 50% penalty on top of your ordinary income tax.

Seriously, 50%?! How can they do that?

They make the rules, they change the rules. What is more damaging to your financial future is not only the market volatility but that you have a silent partner in your retirement. The IRS.

Joe, going back to your return, you mentioned initially that you thought you were getting a 10% return on your money. Were you happy with that percentage?

Definitely, who wouldn't?

Ok, I am going to pick on you Wendy.

Awesome.

I promise to be nice but I have a question. Which would you rather have? An average rate of return of 25% or a compounded 2% rate of return.

I want to say 25 but something tells me that I am wrong.

Here is the thing, people talk about averages and rates of return but the issue is the volatility.

What do you mean?

I mean that if you gave me $100,000 to invest and I could guarantee you a 25% average rate of return (ROR), would you be happy?

I would.

What if I told you that if you chose the compounded guaranteed 2% you would have more?

See, I knew that was coming!

I did set you up for that and I can prove that it works.

Year 1 100,000 x 100% =200,000
Year 2 100,000 x -50% = 100,000
Year 3 100,000 x 100%= 200,000
Year 4 100,000 x -50% = 100,000

So here is how it works, in year 1 you got a 100% ROR, but in year 2 we lost 50%, and year 3 we earn 100% but lose 50% in year 4. We start with $100,000 and end with $100,000, and actually after broker fees and inflation, you probably have around $89,000. Are you happy?

NO! But you said I would make 25%

You did. Take just the ROR's 100-50+100-50=100 divide by 4 years and your average is 25%, why aren't you happy?

Because I didn't make any money!

But Wendy, the market did an average of 25%!

I get your point.

Good, now let's look at the 2% return.

100,000 x 2% = 102,000
102,000 x 2% = 104,040
104040 x 2% = 106,120
106120 x 2% = 108,243

Going with a smaller percentage but not having the volatility wins.

Interesting.

Ok. I need to address something else. You mentioned that in your retirement years that you would be in a lower tax bracket. How does that work?

I don't know, that is just what they say.

They?

You know what I mean.

I do. but I want to be in a much higher tax bracket when I retire.

Really? Why?

Because it means that I actually have money!

Rusty?

Yes Wendy?

What is a Financial Sherpa?

In due time my dear, in due time.

Chapter 11

So what are your options then?

We were hoping you could tell us!

I will, but I want to help teach you to think, not just swallow what I cooked. What are some other options?

Real Estate? CD's? Gold?

All great ideas guys, but remember to put them on trial for their life. So let's do that. But first, I have another story to tell.

A tale of 3 buckets.

When it comes to investing, everyone basically has 3 different buckets of money from which to choose. The first bucket is the taxable bucket. Taxes on this money will range (currently) from 15 to 39.6% and your concerns with this bucket would be mainly to keep pace with inflation. They are short term investments and typically have the lowest rate of return. These would be CD's, Money Market accounts, Savings accounts, and Stocks.

The second bucket is the tax deferred bucket. This is potentially the most volatile bucket, not only due to market fluctuations but also because no one knows where taxes will be when they retire. These are long term investments and consist of 401k's, IRA's, Pensions, Annuities, SEP's, & SIMPLE's. This bucket is also taxed at the highest percentage which is currently 39.6% on the high end.

The third bucket is the tax free bucket. Our issues here are that higher income earners don't qualify for a ROTH IRA, Municipal Bonds are performing at a paltry 2% (if they pay), 529 plans are pigeon holes and getting your money out of them are a challenge at best.

That leaves Life Insurance. Have you ever considered life insurance part of your financial plan? If you haven't you might be missing out.

Wait Rusty, I read a book that told me life insurance was a horrible investment.

I know that book!

You do?

I sure do Joe, and I would have to agree that as a stand-alone product, it performs at a mediocre level. However, if you put it into your portfolio and use it as a "tool" and not a "set it and forget it" product, you will find that it can be an amazing income generator. As a matter of fact, probably one of the best in the marketplace.

Really?

I have no doubt of this whatsoever. I have clients that are successfully combating inflation with this tool. They are safely earning far more money in this than in CDs or money markets. Yet it is almost as liquid as cash and can be your permission slip to spend down your retirement and still leave your family with the money. It is a self-completion to your plan if you were to die prematurely and has no limits to what a creative mind can do with it. Last, but certainly not least, life insurance has some tax advantages as well.

Sounds too good to be true.

It's not, it has its limitations but if you know that going in and buy the right policy from a company that is structured properly, you can do some incredible things with it. And remember, just like everything else, we need to put this on trial for its life.

I would love to hear more.

Chapter 12

Rusty?

Yes Wendy?

I am getting a little overloaded here. It seems like everything we thought we knew was a lie.

Wendy, let me clarify. I don't want to give you the impression that everything you have done or are doing is wrong. That is not my intent, and it simply isn't true. All I am trying to do is show you what you have so that you can see where you are headed. Because, be careful where you are headed...

We might end up where we are going?

You got it Joe!

What does that mean exactly?

Ok Wendy, let's look at that statement. Be careful where you are headed, you may end up where you are going. This is simply a warning that I use to keep myself in check. A barometer of sorts.

Are you getting philosophical here, or religious?

Actually neither. There are some parallels to that statement in the Bible but I don't think you came here for a sermon.

What parallels? I am curious.

I have these marked in my Bible and it says in Proverbs 27 to consider the state of your flocks and give attention to your herds. Another would be in Proverbs 24. I passed by the field of the sluggard and by the vineyard of the man lacking sense and behold it was completely overgrown with thistles. Its surface was covered with nettles and its stone wall was broken down, when I saw I reflected upon it, I looked and received instruction.

All Solomon was saying in these proverbs is what I am saying by my statement about being careful where you are headed, you may end up where you are going. It simply means that you should be reviewing your financial plan periodically and being sure that you are still on target for your goal. You have to be ready to make necessary changes as needed.

I guess that makes sense, but I don't have time to constantly be reviewing this stuff. That is why I hire a professional to help me.

Joe, I understand what you are saying but I need to provide you with some guidance, fatherly advice if you will. Are you open?

Yes.

Are you sure?

That is why we are here!

Good, and Wendy, you are my witness that he asked for this.

I sure am.

Joe, that is the biggest lie you could ever tell yourself. This is exactly how you got yourself in this position. If you don't take ownership of this process, then my work is done. I have fired clients in the past and I am about to fire you.

Wait! Wait!!

No Joe, let me finish.

Ok.

I am NOT trying to start an argument here, but if we are ever going to be successful in our working relationship, you had better hear me and hear me good. This is YOUR plan, this is YOUR future and this is about leaving YOUR legacy. I am not going to sit here and let you bow out on this. I am a professional and I know my profession, but this is your responsibility. I want to help but I can't do it for you. This is going to take sacrifice and commitment on your part. If you cannot agree to this, then our time is done.

No, I get it Rusty.

Do you really?

I think I do. You are telling me that I can't put all of this on you. That I have responsibility here too.

NO!

Huh?

I am saying the responsibility is ALL on you Joe! Listen, I need you to get this, I cannot and will not work with someone who wants to place blame on someone else.

I wasn't.

Yes you did, you said that you don't have time for this and that is why you are hiring a professional. Let me take this down a notch or two and put it another way. Do you ever go to the doctor?

Yes.

And if the doctor tells you that you have high cholesterol and that you need to watch your diet, but you don't have time to constantly be watching what you eat, did hiring that professional do you ANY good?

I guess not.

Good, so as you can see, this is about a financial diet. Just like you told me about cutting back on Starbucks, yet we need to go forward on this journey together with an understanding that it is my job to help guide you but it is not my job to keep you accountable.

Ok, I get it. Wow, guess I didn't expect to get spanked today.

Ha ha.

Wendy, he asked for it, didn't he?

He sure did...*with a smile on her face.*

Joe, I hope you know that I am passionate about what I do, and I genuinely care for people, otherwise I wouldn't be in this business. And sometimes it requires tough love.

Rusty let me ask you if I picked up what you are putting down. You are saying that you are willing to help us build a financial plan, but it is our responsibility to review it and make sure it's working.

You are correct but there is one other commitment we need.

What is that?

That we agree to get together on a regular basis so that we can be sure that my recommendations today are still valid and effective in 5 years.

That makes sense. Weird thing is that I have never had an advisor tell me that we had to meet regularly.

Well I am. I know that things change, life changes, people change and I am not going to have you angry about a decision that was made a decade ago. I need to be in your life so that when there are changes, we can address them. Fair enough?

Yes.

Wendy?

Yes.

Good.

Hey Rusty, can you talk to Joe about helping out with the laundry?

Laughter.

Chapter 13

Let me ask you a question.

Go ahead Wendy.

My cousin goes to her bank for financial advice and the have all of her stuff. Her checking, savings, investments. Is that wrong? Should I talk to her?

Is she happy at her bank?

I don't know.

Well that would be my first question, because we can't fix a problem that others don't see.

True.

But since you brought up banks, let me ask you question. What do banks sell?

What do they sell?

Yes, what does a bank do?

Well I think that they loan money and pay you to save with them.

Partially true, but why are they the biggest buildings in town?

I don't know.

Well it is simple. Banks understand money. Banks originated when there was a need to exchange currencies, so that a traveler could go to another country and be able to purchase food, lodging and the like. And to help with exchange rates, since they change and can be somewhat confusing, like how many pesos can you get for a dollar.

Interesting.

But what does your bank do for you today?

Well we have a checking account there...

That they charge you for.

True, we have a savings account there, we used them to buy our car and our last house.

Ok, so you have used them quite a bit.

Yes.

Let me ask you my question again, what do they sell?

I don't really know, never thought about it, money?

Yes YOUR money, they don't have anything to sell! They are taking your money, and giving you a nominal amount of interest, then they lend your money to someone else and charge them a higher interest rate.

I guess we never thought about that.

Most people don't Joe, but here is the interesting thing. They have a sign on the front door, CD rates as high as 1.4% and a sign on the other door, Auto loans as low as 5%. Whose money are they lending?

Mine!

Exactly. And not only that but, due to the fractional banking system, they can lend out your money up to 10 times.

What?

Yes, they are legally allowed to leverage your money out up to 10 times their reserves. But what has always bothered me is I give them my money to save, but when I need money I have to pay for my money!

I guess I haven't thought about that.

Welcome to the crowd. Would you be interested in being able to become your own bank?

Who wouldn't?

Now if what I haven't told you didn't bother you, I want to see if what I am about to show you will. Both of you look at these calculations with me and if you have any questions, or get lost just stop me, ok?

Ok...*in unison.*

What is the difference between rate and volume concerning interest rates?

No idea.

Ok let's say you are interested in a nice new truck and you would like to borrow some money in order to be able to buy it. You find the right truck it's a great deal and all you need is $50,000.

I'm in!

Slow down Wendy, we have math to do here.

Sorry Rusty, *Ha ha.*

Ok, so you go to the bank for a $50,000 loan and they are going to charge you a 6% interest rate for 6 years. Here is what that looks like.

$50,000 x 6% for 72 months your payment would be $828.64 per month. The total amount of money you would pay back would be $59662.40. The cost to borrow $50k would be $9662.40. That's$ 59662.40-$50,000. Make sense?

Sure.

Ok so let's consider something. Your banker has sold you an interest rate of 6% APR annual percentage rate, correct?

Yes.

Ok, so let's break down our equation a little further. If the cost of money is $9662.40, that is the total amount interest paid to borrow the money. If we divide that total by the same 72 months, it would tell us the amount of interest that is in each payment back to the bank. Make sense?

I think.

Ok Wendy, let me elaborate, every time you write a check to the bank and send them your money, part of that money is the repayment of the $50,000 borrowed and the remaining is the interest or the cost of money of $9662.40, that way in 72 months you have a paid off used truck that is worth about $20,000 dollars.

Ugh, that's true.

Yep and the bank has back the $50k the $9600 and they can do this over and over and up to 10X on the same $50,000.

That explains the big buildings.

It does but there more! Sounds like an infomercial doesn't it.

Ha ha.

But there is something that most people don't get, we are sold on the 6% APR, but the banker lives on the volume of each payment.

Is that the 10x?

No actually I need to finish up my calculation. If you pay back $9662.40 in interest over a 72 month period that would be simply $9662.40 / 72= $134.20 so that means that every time you stroke a check to the bank for $828.64 for the truck, $134.20 if it goes to pay just interest.

But isn't that amortized over the loan?

Sure it is, but that isn't the point. Yes the interest is more in the beginning and the principle is in the end, but what I am showing you is the average volume of interest paid on that truck to borrow $50k for a truck. Right.

Yes.

Ok, so if every time you write the check for $828.64, $134.20 goes to pay interest then we can simply divide 134 by the 828 and it tells us the volume of interest in every payment. Do you have any guesses what that is?

Wouldn't it be the 6%?

You would think but actually it is 16.20%, so every check to the bank is an average of 16.20% going to pay interest.

But the amortization...

Hang on Joe, don't get hung up on semantics. We are simply talking about volume vs rate. Here is my point, do you amortize your checking account in accordance to your loan? No, you simply know that every time you make a payment there is principle and interest. So does the banker. He is living on the volume not the rate. He sells you on the rate.

That doesn't seem fair.

Regardless, it is simply something that I feel you need to know to understand money. And the more you know, the better you can use that knowledge to keep money in your pocket.

That's true.

What if I told you that there is a way to keep the truck that's worth $20,000, loan yourself the money so you get to keep the $50k and you can keep the $9600 in interest too!

I'm all for that, Wendy?

Me too!

Chapter 14

Rusty?

Yes Joe.

What do you think about Gold, and Bitcoins? I have been told that they are great investments.

I will answer your question with a question, a trick I learned that from my wife. What do you really know about Gold or Bitcoins?

Not much. I just had a buddy tell me that you could make a lot of money with them.

Is your buddy investing in them?

Don't really know for sure.

Ok, here is an area we should talk about. You hear all the time, and I mean all the time about the latest, greatest way to become a millionaire overnight. But do you actually know anyone who has, personally know them?

No.

Wendy?

No.

Ok, I don't know anyone who is rolling in the dough because of any of them either and if I did I think I would be rather upset that my "friend" didn't want me along for ride to Richey Rich land. Truthfully there always propositions about how to get uber rich and most of them only profit the people selling them, rarely you. I don't see that many ads for gold these days? Do you?

I see a few.

I see them from time to time but what has always made me uneasy about those pitches were they were always throwing in my face how much money I could make or how much money they made. Seems a little too good to be true.

Ya, I'd have to agree.

But here is another way to approach it. As you could imagine in my line of work, there are always snake oil salesmen that are trying to "help my clients". And momma may have raised a dummy but she didn't raise no fool, you get my drift.

I think so.

Well, they had a great sales pitch about how gold is the standard and that when the dollar fails that gold will be the only way to buy and sell. How gold has always been a constant, blah blah blah. But that never settled well with me.

Me neither.

You got you a smart woman there Joe, you should listen to her.

Ya.

Ok, not trying to create marital issues. *Ha ha.* Have you guys lived in Colorado very long?

I moved here in 1983 and Wendy is a native.

So you guys know what it's like to shop at the grocery store after they have forecast a winter storm?

Oh ya, there is nothing on the shelves.

You're right Wendy, and there is even less on the shelves if there is an actual storm which they are only right about 10% of the time forecasting, am I right.

Chuckling

That's true.

Ok, can you imagine what it would be like to take your gold bar into the grocery store to shave off some gold (if you made it in the store without being robbed), but you are going to try to shop after the dollar has failed, there is no way for anyone to get food and you don't think there will be rioting and looting? I highly doubt that your gold is going to get you too far.

I guess that's about right.

So Joe, to answer your question, I feel that gold can be a great asset to own, but I don't think you are going to get rich overnight on it. If you look at the history of gold, there really isn't much of a story there. You really have to time it just right in order to cash in.

As far as bitcoins, don't know much about them so I stay away. But I want to be transparent with you two about something because I feel that it will help you.

Ok, sounds good.

Several years back, I had a buddy that approached me about a way to make 1% a month on my money or 12% annual return. It was supposed to safe, solid and they wanted me to talk about being a distributor and promised me tons of money. Well I got bitten by the greed bug, just didn't realize it. I thought I was buying a solid investment and that it was a smart business decision. But anytime it sounds too good to be true...

Ya, it usually is.

Where were you Joe when I needed to hear that?

Sorry. *Ha ha*

So I took my life savings and invested in a private placement called factoring.

Factoring?

Yes Wendy, it is a legitimate business but usually handled by major institutions like a Wells Fargo bank, but this private placement was run by a local millionaire.

What exactly is it?

It's designed to help out smaller companies that are strapped for cash either because they are a startup or due to poor financial management.

That doesn't sound too promising if they are poor money managers.

Again, Wendy, where were you? Anyway, the plan was simple, you have a company we will call it a landscaping company. They get a contract with a corporation to mow the grass at the company's campuses. This company has several employees, all who work on an hourly basis and get paid on a weekly or bi weekly pay schedule. But when the work is done, you submit to the corporation a bill for services rendered and that bill has to go through the Accounts Payable department. This can take 30 to 90 days to process, but I highly doubt that your employees can or will wait 90 days for their paycheck, so what does the company owner do? He can use factoring. A private placement lends the business owner a portion of the total amount due for that bill. Let's say the bill is $15000, so you loan him 3% up front with your accounts receivable as collateral. He can use to money for whatever but usually for gas for the mowers, supplies, materials, whatever and then he gets the remaining and then when the bill is paid, he gets 94 to 96% of the total bill paid to him. So all in all he gets 97 to 99% of his total receivables. He likes it because it gives him cash to work with and his employees like it because they get a paycheck. And the private placement likes it because they get 1 to 3% return on their money every month. That's a total annual return of 12 to 36%, not bad huh.

That sounds fantastic.

Well as Paul Harvey would say, here is the rest of the story.

Uh oh.

Uh oh, is right Wendy, because it was a private placement there wasn't anyone watching the hen house, only the foxes and they went belly up, so everyone's money disappeared.

That's horrible.

It is Wendy, but the worst part was that I knew some seniors that were taken for their entire retirement accounts.

Oh my gosh.

And I was lucky.

Lucky?

Yes Joe, lucky because I was young and I could afford to, or better said, had time to earn back my money. It was a costly education into the world of finance. But it made me realize that I was responsible for what happened, not them.

How were you responsible?

Wendy, no one held a gun to my head. I got suckered in because I was greedy. I didn't realize my greed until it was too late, but regardless I had to take ownership for my situation.

Now I know why you were so tough on me earlier.

You right Joe but I also know you have broad shoulders and can take it. It is better that you eat some humble pie now because my pie was really expensive.

How much did you lose?

Too much. Doesn't matter if it was a dollar, it was all because of me trying to take a shortcut and guys I can tell you right now, there are none.

Sure there are guys that made fortunes in the tech boom, but there are many more that lost everything. It just isn't worth it. So if you take nothing else from this, please listen to an old Okie, be smart not greedy.

I noticed an accent.

Been here for decades but every so often the redneck still comes out.

We won't hold that against you.

Thank you Wendy, you are too sweet.

laughter.

Chapter 15

Rusty, are you ever going to tell us why Aaron calls you the financial Sherpa?

Well I guess I could, but let me say something first. Do you both agree that this meeting wasn't at all what you were expecting?

Definitely.

Without a doubt.

Good, because that is the intent. My goal isn't to sell you a product. Products are useless and dangerous without a plan.

So what do you sell?

I don't, I provide a strategy, or a plan and use products to help make that plan perform.

But we really don't have all that much money Rusty. It isn't like we are Donald Trump.

But what you are missing is that regardless of whether you make $70,000 or $7 million, you need a plan. A plan that is designed to perform when taxes go up and when they go down. A plan that performs even if you are not in the picture any longer. A plan that will help you achieve your goals even in the lean times.

So what you are saying is that you are the Sherpa that gets us to the top of the mountain?

No Wendy.

You're not? I'm confused.

I am a financial Sherpa and if all I ever do is get you to the top of the mountain, I have failed you miserably. Let me tell you one more story.

You may have seen the chart in your financial planner's office that shows if you had put $1 in the stock market in 1912 that you would have a ridiculous amount of money today. But let me ask you a question, aside from Warren Buffet, how many individuals do you know that have actually made a ton of money in the stock market? Most people don't make the rates of return that are suggested, and even more lose money. The returns that are suggested in the market are not what the individual person earns. But what even more of an issue is, getting off that mountain.

Approximately 6000 people have attempted to climb Mount Everest, 440 were successful, and 183 have died trying to climb Everest. What is staggering is that of the 183 that died, 85% died on the descent. What that tells me is that they focused mostly on the pinnacle, but that is only half the story. What about getting off Mount Retirement?

Some of the issues that you face are:

- *Outliving your money*
- *Losing your nest egg to Medicaid*
- *Dying before you can retire*

My point is simply this, my job is more important getting you off the mountain. It really doesn't matter how much money you have if you can't spend it due to fear of taxes or afraid you won't have enough to be able to leave a legacy.

Is this why Aaron was talking to me about the senior market?

It is Joe, and I feel that you could be a great person to help others because you care about something other than yourself.

Is my little Joey going to be Financial Sherpa?

That's a decision you both will make, Wendy. But I want you to know that a Sherpa is as focused getting you off that mountain as he is going up. If you get sloppy, or careless you die. If you run out of oxygen, you die. If you run out of energy...

You die.

Exactly Joe. There is another side to this mountain that we haven't discussed. Like how seniors don't know that CD's can trigger additional taxation on their social security. Or how to utilize a reverse mortgage in your plan to offset the down years of the market to shelter your IRA. And so much more.

Wow!

That is an appropriate response Wendy, but for this meeting we will focus on making sure you guys make it to the pinnacle and make sure that we are setting up a plan to get you off that mountain too!

Conclusion

This book is fiction but with many parallels to my real life. The fact of the matter is that most people really don't understand how money works and it is costing them dearly. Hopefully I have made you think. If so, I have done my job.

This book is not intended to provide any financial advice or to promote any product. It is not intended to provide any tax or legal advice. Please consult a professional before making any decisions regarding these areas.

My goal isn't to sell you anything but to educate, and once you have your eyes opened you can make smarter and better choices. I hate the things I see and hear about seniors losing their hard earned savings or being swindled out of their money. I had to see anyone lose their money, whether it is a millionaire ball player or a thousand-aire insurance agent. I hope you found this educational.

If you are interested in learning more about any of the things discussed in this book or have other questions. Feel free to reach out to me at jpvsr@icloud.com

www.ingramcontent.com/pod-product-compliance
Lightning Source LLC
Chambersburg PA
CBHW070919180526
45168CB00005B/2073